TRACTATUS PHILOSOPHICUS TAO

A short treatise on the *Tao Te Ching* of Lao Tzu

KEITH SEDDON

Seekers on the spiritual path will find that Lao Tzu's classic of philosophical Taoism, the *Tao Te Ching*, continues to inspire and instruct. Explore the mysterious Tao in this playful and whimsical pastiche of Ludwig Wittgenstein's *Tractatus Logico-Philosophicus* as you meditate on Lao Tzu's message.

Avoids excess, extremes, and extravagance. Embrace the oneness of the Tao, become like an uncarved block, and return to simplicity.

Keith Seddon is a freelance academic and author. He is Professor of Philosophy at Warnborough College Ireland.

By the same author

Lao Tzu: Tao Te Ching

Learning the Tao: Chuang Tzu as Teacher

The Stoic Fragments of Epictetus
[forthcoming]

An Outline of Cynic Philosophy: Antisthenes of Athens and Diogenes of Sinope in Diogenes Laertius Book Six
[forthcoming]

A Summary of Stoic Philosophy: Zeno of Citium in Diogenes Laertius Book Seven

Stoic Serenity: A Practical Course on finding Inner Peace

Epictetus' Handbook and the Tablet of Cebes: Guides to Stoic Living

Time: A Philosophical Treatment

TRACTATUS PHILOSOPHICUS TAO

A short treatise on the

Tao Te Ching of Lao Tzu

by

Keith Seddon

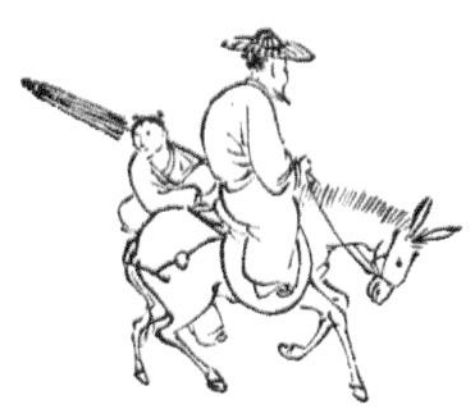

Lulu

First published 2008
by Keith Seddon
at Lulu
www.lulu.com

Typeset in Constantia and Calibri

ISBN 978–0–955–68445–6 (paperback)

For all my good friends, with special apologies to Ludwig Wittgenstein (whom of course I never knew).

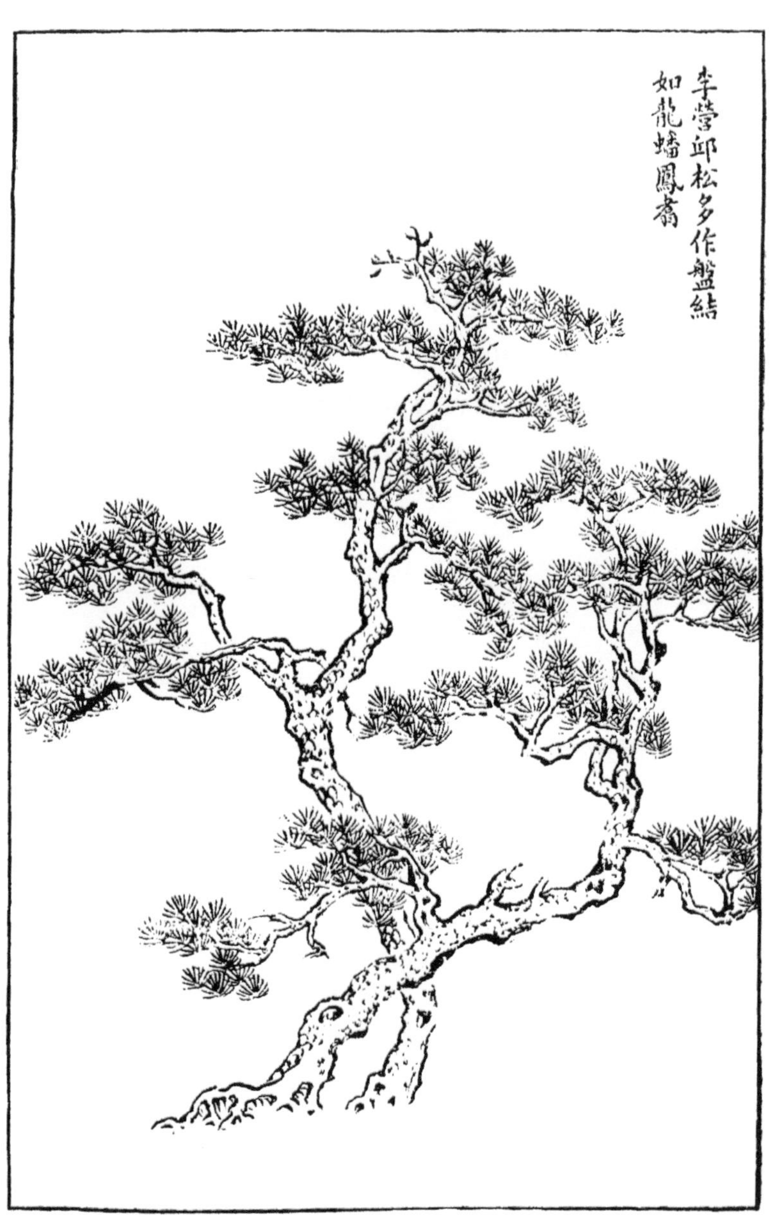
李營邱松多作盤結
如龍蟠鳳翥

CONTENTS

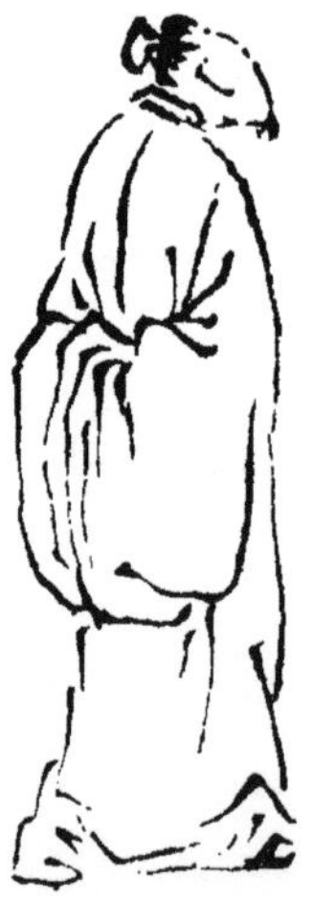

PREFACE

This little book attempts to reconstruct the philosophical Taoism that is contained in the ancient Chinese classics of Lao Tzu, Chuang Tzu and Lieh Tzu into a coherent whole, methodologically structured around key Taoist notions. Since all these notions need to be before the mind simultaneously for any one of them (and for Taoist philosophy as a whole) to make sense, the reader is advised to pass through this book, back and forth, feeding their comprehension and nurturing their understanding. In this way, care for your own thoughts, just as the Tao nourishes all things.

Unlike most other works treating philosophical topics, this book does not attempt to provide arguments for its conclusions (indeed, there is no obvious way of determining which statements are its conclusions). Rather, it simply makes suggestions (not conclusions or even assertions) which are followed by remarks intended to provide clarifying explanations – and perhaps not explanations, but rather explorations. Its task is modest: it suggests that there is a source of being (the being that you and I and everything else existing in the universe enjoys) and elucidates this notion. Doing this will involve looking at some metaphysical and ontological notions. But having done that, Taoist philosophy maintains that in consequence of appreciating such ideas, certain moralities (private and public) arise. The person who realises this, and who puts this morality into practice, is called by the Taoist, the Sage.

The Sage 'holds to the oneness of the Tao' and models himself on the Tao. The more Sages there are, the more light there is in the world. As the number of Sages declines, darkness fills the world. And alas, the world is full of darkness. It is not my aim in writing this little book to convince anyone of anything; but my hope is that it will contribute to the making of Sages who can push back the darkness.

Most commentators refer to the Tao using the definite article 'the', as I am doing now. Yet the Tao is something which strictly speaking cannot be referred to at all. 'The' when used in the expression 'the Tao' cannot function as it does in the sentences: 'Bring me the pen.' 'Is that the taxi already?' The Tao is not something that can be picked out, since it does not lie in a context which is greater than itself. There is nothing to pick it out from. All this is meant as something of an excuse to recommend that you try re-reading some of the following sections which mention the Tao by deliberately missing out all instances of 'the', and substituting 'Tao' for 'the Tao'. Convince yourself that 'Tao' functions like 'infinity', that 'the Tao' is no less nonsensical than 'the infinity'.

Note on the decimal numbering system

The system of decimal numbers assigned to the individual sections in the text that follows is modelled on the system used by Ludwig Wittgenstein in his *Tractatus Logico-Philosophicus* (which, quite obviously has been my inspiration for exploring the Tao in the way that I have). Sections 1.1, 1.2, 1.3, etc. expand on section 1; sections 2.21, 2.22, 2.23, etc. expand on section 2.2; and similarly, 2.231, 2.232, 2.233 expand on 2.23, and so forth.

Quotations from the *Tao Te Ching* are taken from my own translation, published by Lulu in 2006.

Keith Seddon

Hertfordshire, England
June 2008

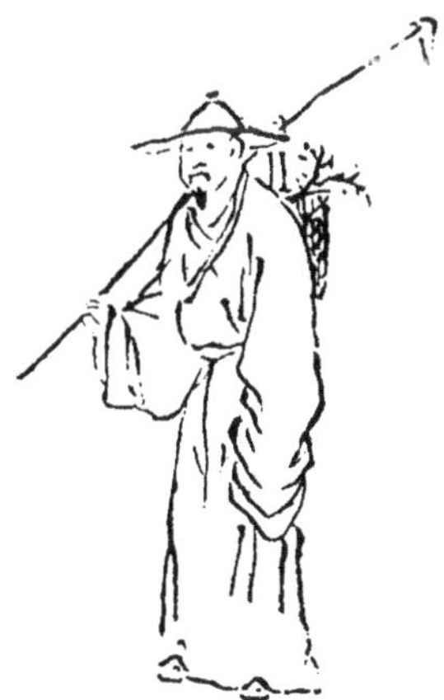

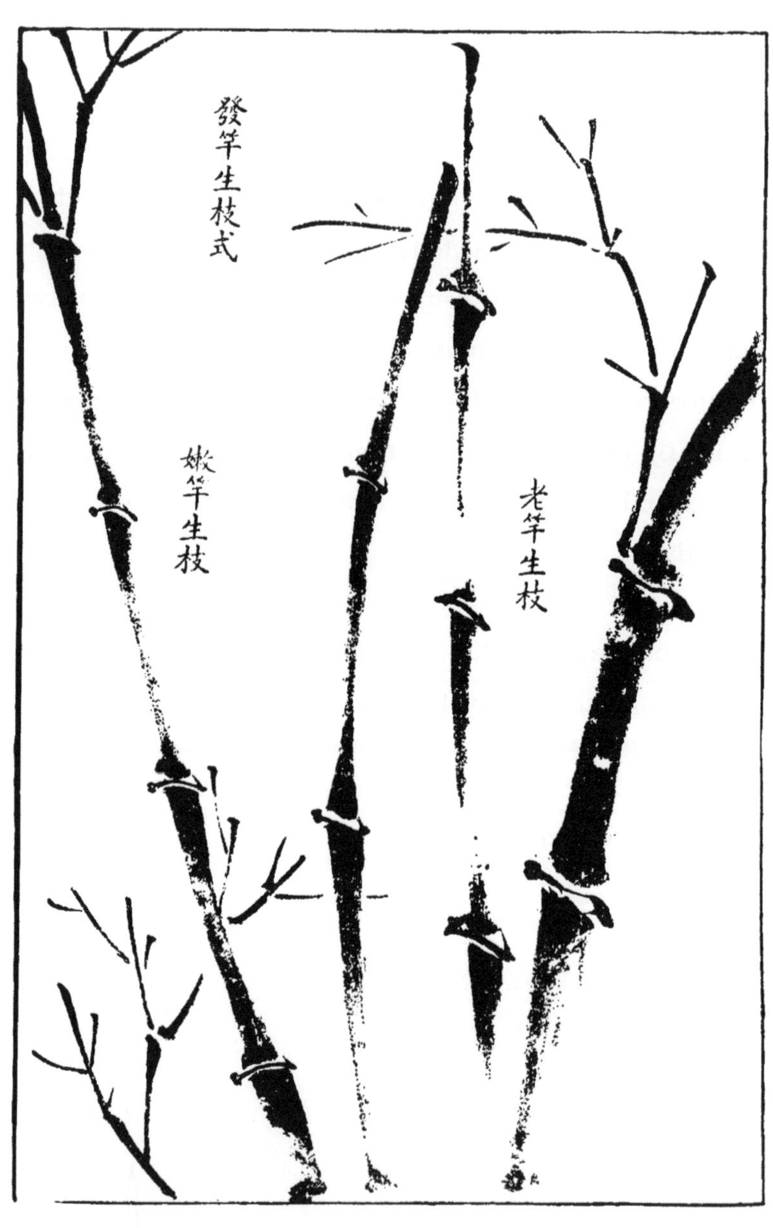
發竿生枝式
嫩竿生枝
老竿生枝

TRACTATUS PHILOSOPHICUS TAO

1 **The Tao is all that is the case.**

1.01 It is the totality of everything.

1.02 It embraces all possible states of affairs.

1.1 The Tao gives rise to the world of phenomena.

1.11 It gives rise to all things but also to the relations in which things stand towards each other. (Is it contingent that things stand in relation towards each other? Can we imagine a possible world in which there are things but *no relations* between things?)

1.12 When people can appreciate beauty in beautiful things, this is because there is already ugliness with which it can be contrasted. When people can appreciate the good in people, this is because there are already evil people with whom they can be contrasted.

Easy and difficult rely upon each other; long and short are dependent upon each other; high and low contrast with each other; before and after follow each other.

Being and non-being arise together. (See 1.521; see *Tao Te Ching* 2.)

1.2 Experiences are of the world, never of the Tao.

1.21 Only constituent parts of the world can be experienced, never the world as a whole.

1.22 The Tao cannot be experienced.

1.23 It is not logically possible to have an experience of the relation between the Tao and the world (in contrast to the possibility of having an experience of any number of possible relations between things *in* the world; for instance, someone can be aware in one experience that this stick is longer than another stick).

1.2301 Logically it is not possible to have an experience of that which is the *source* of our experiences. Scientists would have us believe that what gives rise to our experiences is the behaviour of atoms and molecules. These things cannot be experienced directly (as a cat can be experienced directly – you open your eyes and there it is): they are merely *ideas*, conceptions employed in a theory. Why should we believe that this theory is correct or that the models it uses attach to the way things really are? Atoms and molecules are elements in a picture or a model. They cannot be *identical* with what really exists.

Believing that atoms doing what they are purported to do gives rise to our experiences can by analogy be compared with our believing that the sound of barking coming from a shed is produced by a dog. But we can never 'get behind' our experiences to see if it is atoms that give rise to them, so in the analogy we must suppose that we are unable to get into the shed to see if there really is a dog there. But we could be wrong about the dog. Our hearing the barking can be explained by other theories: there may be a tape-recorder in the shed, or a person imitating a dog, or maybe what we hear as barking is produced by an entirely different sort of creature, nothing like a dog.

Atoms are ideas. There is no reason for believing that they actually exist.

1.231 Looked for, it cannot be seen: it is not visible. Listened for, it cannot be heard: it makes no sound. Grasped at, it cannot be held: it is not tangible. Go to meet it, and you will find no beginning. Follow after it and you will find no end. (*Tao Te Ching* 14)

1.232 Tao is invisible and intangible. It is invisible and intangible, yet within is form [the form of all things which it gives rise to]. It is intangible and invisible, yet within is substance [the substance of all the things which it gives rise to]. (*Tao Te Ching* 21)

1.3 The Tao is the source of all things.

1.301 An uncarved block serves as a picture of the Tao.

1.31 In its unfathomable depths arise the Ten Thousand Things. (*Tao Te Ching* 4)

1.3101 When the uncarved block is split into pieces, the Ten Thousand Things are brought into being.

1.3202 When you can comprehend the picture of the oneness of the uncarved block at one and the same time as seeing the block split into the Ten Thousand Things, then you have comprehended the relation between the Tao and the Ten Thousand Things.

1.4 The existence of the world is dependent upon the Tao.

1.41 The Tao is not the *cause* of the world.

1.411 'Cause' and 'effect' are concepts that apply *in* the world: they cannot be applied to anything that is not a constituent part of the world, and therefore not with regard to anything to which the world stands in relation (the Tao).

1.42 The relationship between the Tao and the world can be elucidated by analogy. The blobs of paint adhering to a canvas are not *themselves* the picture, but when viewed from an appropriate distance are *seen as* a picture. The blobs of paint 'produce' or 'give rise to' the picture. The nature that the Tao actually has is something that we cannot (logically) be acquainted with, but whatever its true nature is, it empowers the Tao to produce, or give rise to, the world.

1.421 There is no way to decide whether the nature that the Tao has results necessarily or contingently in there being a world.

1.5 The Tao is nameless. (*Tao Te Ching* 1, 32, 37)

1.501 In attempting to name the Tao, you cannot name the unnamed Tao which was there before your attempt began. The Tao is nameless in the sense that it cannot (logically) be named, since in the very act of applying a name, what you had hoped to name has changed into something else – that is, from an unnamed thing to a named thing. What is true about the Tao, that it is unnamed, becomes false when someone attempts to name it. Its attributes, in this respect, change.

1.5011 Similarly, it is logically impossible to grasp the Tao in thought, or explain it in language.

1.502 The Tao that can be put in words is not the ever-abiding Tao; the name that can be named is not the ever-abiding name. (*Tao Te Ching* 1)

1.503 Anything that can be spoken of is not the Tao. Anything that can be thought about is not the Tao. Even the Sage cannot explain what it is that is referred to in this book.

1.51 When we name something or someone, it must be possible to associate a thought with what is being named. Otherwise we are just inventing words that appear to stand in the place of names in our statements, but do not in fact name anything. (It is a person who names, and not the word itself – written or spoken – which is used merely as an instrument to do the naming. Similarly, a spanner cannot by itself loosen a nut. Names are like tools which can do work only when they are used by someone.)

The thought with which it must be possible to associate what is named, serves to distinguish the thing named from its background. For instance, in the kitchen, 'teapot' serves to distinguish from everything else in the kitchen that object referred to as 'teapot'. (Similarly, proper names serve to distinguish the people or objects that are named from all the other people and things in the world.)

The term 'Tao' cannot function like other nouns (for example, 'teapot'), or like proper names, since there is nothing beyond the Tao from which it can be distinguished. The Tao has no background.

1.511 Think of it this way. The subject can be distinguished against a background (think of a white teapot against a black backdrop), and a background can be distinguished from a subject that stands before it.

1.5111 But there is nothing against which both subject *and* background *taken together* can be distinguished.

1.52 The Tao is that through which all things come into being – hence the Tao itself cannot be a thing. It is transcendent to 'thingness'. We cannot say what it is or what its properties are, but we can say what it does: it brings things into being and sustains them (in a logical sense) throughout their histories. We cannot identify any mechanism by which it does this, and we cannot say why it should do such a thing. It does: that's all that can be said.

1.521 The Tao is beyond being and non-being. But in so far as the Tao is what underlies all things-which-exist, it itself cannot be a thing-which-exists, so is called 'non-being'.

1.6 The Tao accomplishes all things through non-action.

1.601 Non-action is neither action nor not-action.

1.61 The Tao never acts, yet nothing is left undone. (*Tao Te Ching* 37)

1.62 To act through non-action is to act spontaneously and effortlessly.

1.7 The world is continuously changing.

1.71 That which yields will overcome. That which bends will be straight. That which is empty will be filled. That which wears out will be renewed. He who has little will gain more. He who has much will be perplexed. (*Tao Te Ching* 22)

1.8 The Tao is unchanging.

It is silent and fathomless, formless yet complete. Inexhaustible and pervading everywhere, it may be thought of as the Mother of the Ten Thousand Things. (See *Tao Te Ching* 25)

1.81 The Tao has been likened to a vessel that can be poured from but never exhausted. (*Tao Te Ching* 4)

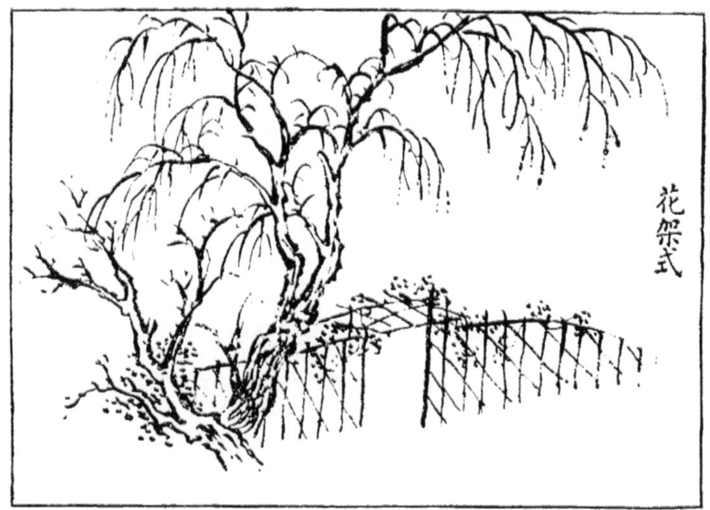

2 The Tao is not God.

2.01 The Tao is transcendent. It cannot be said to exist *in* reality, since it produces reality, and it is what that which is real depends upon for its being. It is not extended in space, and it does not endure through time.

2.02 The Tao cannot be differentiated into parts.

2.03 There is only one Tao.

2.04 The Tao is not knowable.

2.1 The Tao is not conscious.

2.11 Although the Tao brings all things into being and brings each to completion, this is not done intentionally, or with any purpose in mind. It just happens, but not because something or other is *done* to bring it about.

2.1101 Only creatures that are self-conscious (that is, not just conscious, but conscious that they are) can act with purpose or have an intention.

It may seem that some creatures act with a purpose (as for instance when a bird builds a nest), but this is simply to attribute human characteristics to a completely different sort of creature. *If* a person was making something like a bird's nest, we would suppose that this person had some purpose in mind. We can discover the purpose by asking them 'Why are you doing that?' This person would have an awareness of what would count as successfully completing the project. They would have an awareness of ends which their creation is designed to meet. None of this is the case with the bird. The bird just does build a nest, and that is all we can say about the situation, other than to make factual remarks about how big the nest is, how long it takes to build, what sort of materials are used for its construction, and so forth.

2.2 The Tao cannot be worshipped.

2.21 Prayer directed towards the Tao is futile.

2.3 The Tao is not compassionate.

2.31 To be compassionate is to adopt a certain outlook over someone or something. For some people this would involve having certain feelings. (This could be a logical point, that to be compassionate one *must* be aware that one has this sort of outlook and *must* have appropriate sorts of feelings towards the object of one's compassion – pity, say. Would we say that someone who was not aware that they had adopted this special outlook and who did not have the appropriate sorts of feelings, yet who in all other respects behaved compassionately – who merely had a mysterious disposition to behave compassionately – really is compassionate?) The Tao is not that kind of thing which can have feelings or adopt outlooks. The evil that we see in the world shows that the Tao has no *disposition* to be compassionate. The Tao may not be that sort of thing that can have dispositions. What is the difference in saying that the Tao gives rise to the world, and the Tao has the disposition to give rise to the world?

2.311 When we use the term 'compassionate' we imply several things: perhaps that the compassionate person is better than others, is praiseworthy – that we regard them more highly. If someone is said to be compassionate, this is consistent with their being in different circumstances less compassionate or not compassionate at all.

These implications make no sense if we try to apply the term 'compassionate' to the Tao. But since these implications are part of what we *mean* by 'compassionate', what meaning can it have when applied to the Tao? Well, not its ordinary meaning. So to say that the Tao is compassionate is to say something without meaning.

2.32 Heaven and Earth are impartial; they regard the Ten Thousand Things as Straw dogs. (*Tao Te Ching* 5)

2.321 In ancient Chinese philosophy, Heaven and Earth interact with each other, and in so doing produce the world of phenomena. In this sense they can be identified with the Tao. Heaven is conceived of as active, and acts upon the passive Earth. Heaven is masculine, and Earth is feminine. In terms of yin and yang, Earth is yin, and Heaven is yang. 'Heaven' frequently means simply 'nature' or 'the natural world'. When ancient Chinese philosophy says that all things happen in accord with Heaven, or at Heaven's beckoning, Heaven is seen as the controlling, activating force responsible for everything that happens. Thought of in this way, 'Heaven' appears to be essentially the same as 'the Tao'.

2.322 In ancient China, straw dogs were made to be sacrificial offerings at religious ceremonies. Afterwards, having served their purpose, they would be thrown away and trampled underfoot in the street, or gathered up by poor people to be burnt as fuel. (*Tao Te Ching* 5)

2.33 Similarly, the Tao is not benevolent.

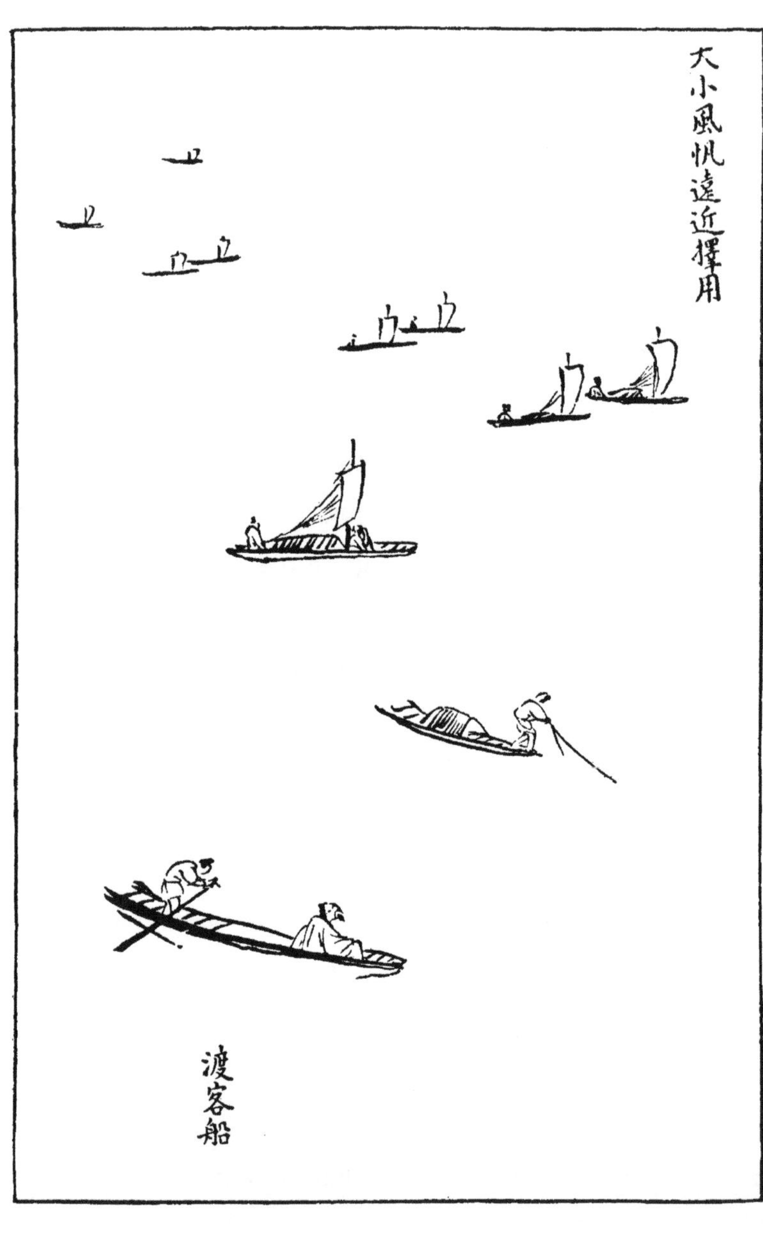
大小風帆遠近擇用
渡客船

3 Through the Tao all things are brought to completion.

3.01 It produces them but does not possess them; accomplishes without taking credit; guides without interfering. (*Tao Te Ching* 51)

3.02 It blunts sharp edges, unties all tangles; it softens the glare and blends with the dust. (*Tao Te Ching* 4) [Dust is a Taoist symbol for the noise and fuss of everyday life.]

3.1 All things return to the source of their being when it is time. (*Tao Te Ching* 16, 34)

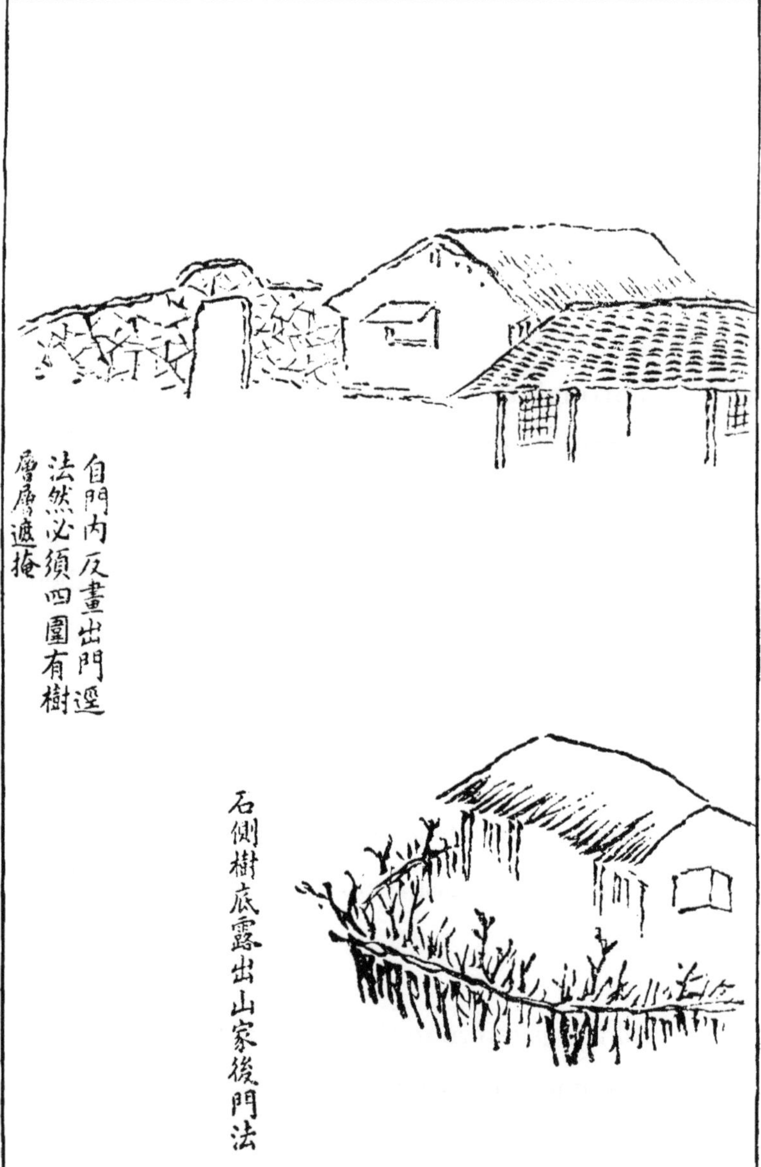
自門内反畫出門逕
法然必須四圍有樹
層層遮掩
石側樹底露出山家後門法

4 The Sage is he who holds to the oneness of the Tao.

4.01 Holding to the oneness of the Tao is what one does when one recognises Tao as the source of all being and its mode of operation.

4.02 The Sage models himself on the Tao.

4.021 Thus he acts spontaneously and effortlessly, accomplishing through non-action. (*Tao Te Ching* 64)

4.0211 Accomplishing through non-action is to dispense with trying, intending, and striving. The Sage does things, but the things he does he does not try, intend, or strive to do.

4.0212 Consciously trying to accomplish something results in failure. The pianist who has perfected a piece, who when playing it tries to be conscious of the movements of each of his fingers will be unable to play on.

He can play the piece. But this is not to say that he does so by trying to move each finger to its proper key at the proper time.

4.1 The Sage sets an example for everyone. (*Tao Te Ching* 22)

4.11 He does not make a great show, therefore he shines out. He does not try to justify himself, and so is distinguished. He does not boast, so he receives merit. He is not arrogant, and so endures. Because he does not compete, no one can compete with him. (*Tao Te Ching* 22)

4.12 He leads by coming last. (*Tao Te Ching* 7)

4.2 The Sage is not conscious that he is a Sage.

4.21 No one can intentionally strive to be a Sage.

4.211 To become a Sage one must periodically remind oneself of how the Sage differs from the ordinary person. One must cease from aiming at things.

4.3 The Sage accomplishes his tasks through non-action, neither possessing what he produces, nor claiming credit. (*Tao Te Ching* 77)

4.301 The Sage does not act as he does out of any interest or desire to satisfy the moral requirements of a higher being (God or Tao – though the Tao is not a 'higher being') or of a code; neither does he act as he does in order to attain harmony with the Tao.

Understanding this is to understand the essence of non-action. The Sage just does act as he does, and just is in harmony with the Tao.

Is there a training of any sort that one can undergo to make this coming about – with regard to oneself – more likely?

4.31 Those who take action, fail. Those who grasp for things, lose them. Therefore the Sage takes no action, yet never fails; he grasps for nothing, yet never loses. (*Tao Te Ching* 64)

4.32 The Sage plans the difficult while it is still easy, accomplishes greatness in small things, deals with things before they happen, puts things in order before chaos sets in. (*Tao Te Ching* 63, 64)

4.321 There are times for forging ahead, and for staying behind; for keeping silent, and for speaking aloud. Some are strong, while others are weak; some rejoice while others lament. (*Tao Te Ching* 29)

4.33 He works without claiming reward, accomplishes without taking credit. He has no desire to display his excellence. (*Tao Te Ching* 77)

4.34 The Sage is cautious, like one crossing a river in winter; hesitant, like one who fears his neighbours; reserved, like one who is a guest; yielding, like ice that is melting; simple, like an uncarved block; open, like a wide valley; obscure, like muddy water. (*Tao Te Ching* 15)

4.4 The Sage does not distinguish between solving a problem and failing to solve a problem, since all that happens arises as the natural unfolding of the Tao – even that circumstance in which a man views something that happens as a problem for him.

4.5 The Sage has dispensed with desire.

4.501 Suffering desire is the worst calamity. Being free from desire, tranquillity is attained.

4.51 When the Sage has money, he spends it wisely, though of course he gives most of it away to the needy. But when the Sage has no money, this is when he is happiest of all.

4.511 This is because having money and desire offers the shortest route to possessions and attachments. Having possessions and attachments is like pulling a curtain across the Tao.

4.5101 The more curtains that are pulled across the Tao, the darker the world becomes.

4.6 The Sage has dispensed with fear.

4.6001 The Sage, holding to Tao, can smile at danger and laugh at adversity.

4.601 Therefore he has no fear of death, for himself or for others.

4.6011 Why lament the passing of the dead? Is it not a fact that for an infinite period before someone was born they had no existence? And is it not a fact that for an infinite period after someone dies they will have no existence? To regard these two facts as a calamity is to regard the natural working of the Tao as a calamity.

Only the foolish and unenlightened are capable of doing this.

4.602 The Ten Thousand Things return to their source at the proper time. Arising from the source of all things is neither good nor bad; returning to the source of all things is neither good nor bad. Yet accepting with joy the endless unfolding of the Tao is better than wishing that things could be other than they are. (*Tao Te Ching* 34)

4.61 When the tree is growing does it think to itself: 'Which way should I grow now? Up, over here? To the left or to the right?' Does it think: 'For how long will I live? For a short time, or for many years? What if the woodcutter should come and cut me down! Woe! Woe! Woe!'

If the tree were to think such things its growth would be stunted. In such a state of anxiety it would lose its leaves by June.

4.62 It is said that in antiquity people lived to great ages, far surpassing the mean spans that men today attain. Might this have been because people in the past were more like trees than men? Without thought they did what was natural for them, unburdened with the need to make decisions or with the fear of their eventual fates.

4.7 Possessions bring misfortune.

4.701 There is no crime greater than having desires. No disaster is greater than not being content with one's lot. The worst misfortune is to be greedy. He who is content with what he has, has enough. (*Tao Te Ching* 46)

4.71 One day the Sage lost all his possessions, but he smiled at his misfortune and went on his way. The rich man lost all his wealth and thought this was the height of calamity. Since Heaven has treated them equally, how is it that one smiles and the other wallows in self-pity?

4.711 This is because misfortune arises from within, not from without.

4.72 It is only by ceasing to seek after life's pleasures that one will find life pleasurable. (*Tao Te Ching* 75)

4.8 The Sage knows when to stop.

4.801 Knowing when to stop is the best piece of wisdom that the Sage possesses. Knowing when to stop, one avoids all danger. (*Tao Te Ching* 32, 44)

4.802 Since the Universe is sacred no improvements can be made. If you try to change it, you will spoil it. (*Tao Te Ching* 29)

4.81 To fill the cup to the brim only makes it more likely that it will overflow: better not to have filled it so much. The finely honed blade, when used, will soon lose its sharpness: why sharpen it to such an extent? Fill the hall with gold and jade, and it will soon be plundered: better not to have amassed such treasure. The man who takes pride in his wealth and honours attracts his own downfall. (*Tao Te Ching* 9)

4.8101 To stop when the task is finished is the Way of Heaven. (*Tao Te Ching* 9)

4.82 He who is courageous in taking action is soon killed. He who is courageous in remaining passive keeps his life. Of the two kinds of courage, one is harmful and the other advantageous. (*Tao Te Ching* 73)

4.9 The Sage avoids excess, extremes, and extravagance. (*Tao Te Ching* 29)

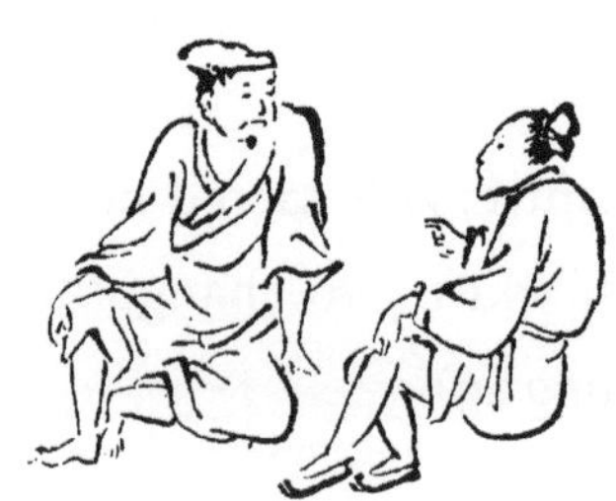

5 That which is contrary to the Tao comes to a swift end.

5.1 Trying to make things do what they would not otherwise be inclined to do anyway leads to disaster.

5.11 The rain falls and the sun shines. Breezes blow and trees grow. Only human beings do things which are unnatural, despite the Sage's warnings. This is because it is the Tao of man to behave unnaturally. Even though disaster is the result, there is nothing that can be done about this.

5.2 Do not be beguiled by desire.

5.21 Mankind strives to accomplish all manner of foolish things contrary to the Tao. This is because people are beguiled by desire and motivated by folly. This is why the men of Tao leave the world and go to live in the mountains and the deserts. There, there are thousands and thousands of them, living in harmony with nature so successfully that no one else has any idea that they exist at all.

Looked for they cannot be seen; called after they make no reply. Watched for they move about invisibly like the wind; listened for they talk in buzzes and whirrs mimicking the cameras which in vain take time-delayed exposures which later reveal just the mountains and the deserts.

5.3 Whosoever searches can find the Tao. If it is possible to find the Tao, is there anything which cannot be found?

5.4 Under Heaven, nothing is softer and weaker than water. Yet nothing is better for attacking the hard and the strong. In time, even the highest mountain range will be worn down to a level plain; even the boulder in the stream will be reduced to a pebble.

5.41 All under Heaven know that the weak overcomes the strong and the soft overcomes the hard. (*Tao Te Ching* 36, 78)

5.42 When the ancients said, 'Yield and overcome,' was that an empty saying? (*Tao Te Ching* 22)

5.421 Yet the Sage despairs that there are none who practise this. (*Tao Te Ching* 78)

5.5 A high wind will not last all morning, and a sudden downpour will not last all day. Why is this? Heaven and Earth have made it so. If Heaven and Earth cannot make things which last forever, how much less is it possible for man? (*Tao Te Ching* 23)

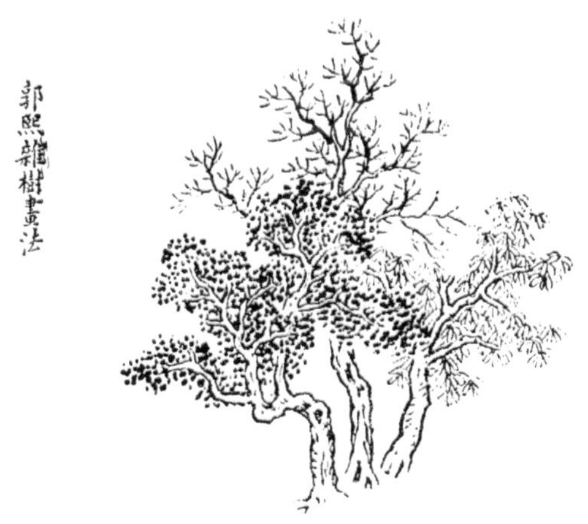

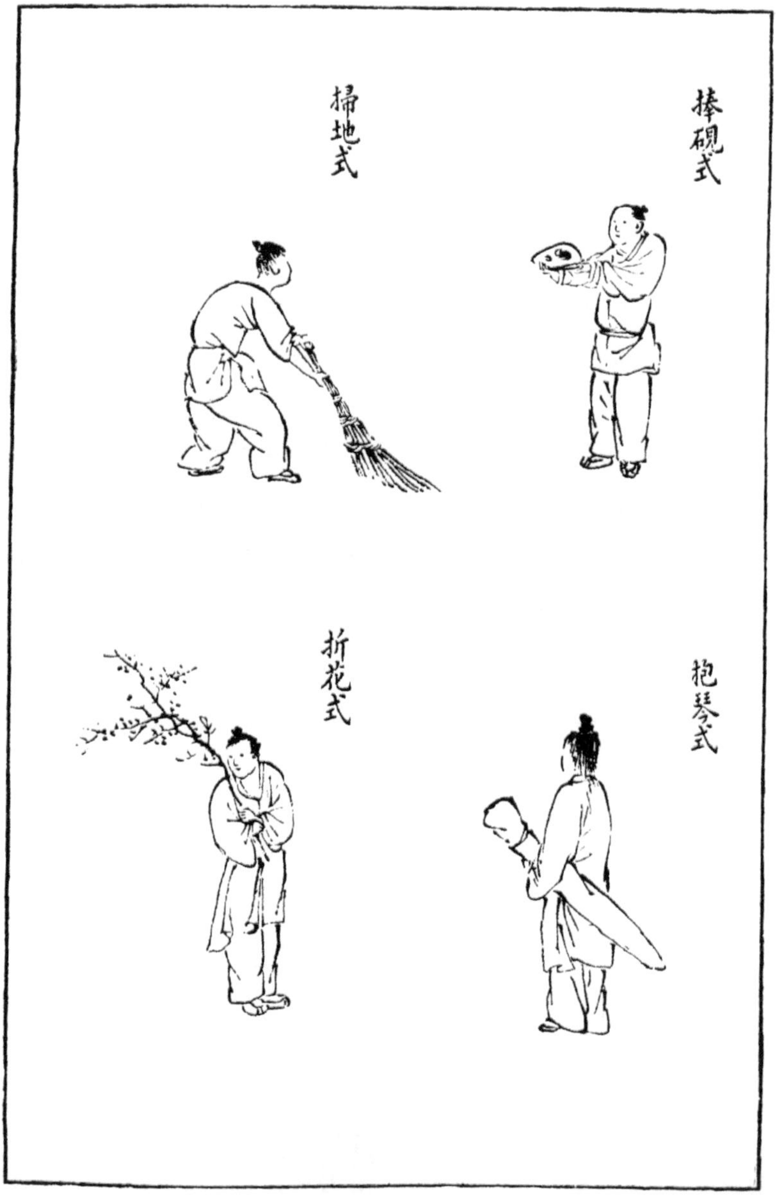

捧硯式

掃地式

抱琴式

折花式

6 The wise ruler is like the Sage, holding to the oneness of the Tao.

6.1 The wise ruler knows when to stop.

6.11 He does what is needed, then stops.

6.2 The wise ruler knows that rules cannot serve his purpose.

6.21 Human beings are naturally disposed to behave in certain ways. So, very generally, either rules are framed which accord with these natural dispositions, and so are never broken, or rules are framed which are not in accord with these natural dispositions, in which case they will be broken frequently. Either way, rules serve no purpose.

6.3 The wise ruler allows the people to follow their natural inclinations. He lets them manage their own domestic affairs for themselves; lets them work according to their own dispositions. Since he does not oppress them, they are not oppressed. (*Tao Te Ching* 72)

6.4 When ruling the people there is nothing better than restraint. (*Tao Te Ching* 59)

6.41 Imposing upon the people will generate resistance.

6.42 If the people prove difficult to rule it is because the rulers interfere too much. (*Tao Te Ching* 75)

6.5 The wise ruler has recourse to war only as a last resort.

6.51 Adopting force will invite resistance. (*Tao Te Ching* 30)

6.52 Weapons are the tools of misfortune; they are not the choice of the wise man, who uses them only when there is no other way, and even then, he acts with calm restraint, and victory is no occasion for rejoicing. (*Tao Te Ching* 31)

6.53 When Tao is present in the world racehorses are taken off to work in the fields. When Tao is absent from the world war-horses are bred in the countryside. (*Tao Te Ching* 46)

6.6 The wise ruler is not extravagant.

6.61 When the court is maintained in lavish splendour, the fields are full of weeds and the granaries are empty. Some wear extravagant clothes and carry sharp swords. They consume food and drink to excess and accumulate more wealth and possessions than they can find use for. This is called robbery and extravagance, and is contrary to Tao. (*Tao Te Ching* 53)

6.7 The best ruler stays in the background, and his voice is rarely heard. When he accomplishes his task, and things go well, the people think it was they who did it by themselves. (*Tao Te Ching* 17)

6.71 So the best rulers are those whom the people hardly know exist. Next come rulers whom the people love and praise. After that come rulers whom the people fear. And the worst rulers are those whom the people despise. (*Tao Te Ching* 17)

6.711 The ruler who does not trust the people will not be trusted by the people. (*Tao Te Ching* 17)

6.8 When the whole world attains the Tao there will be no need any more to mention the Tao.

6.9 What we have discussed in this book is not the Tao, but merely a feeble glimmer of a shadow of what the Tao is really like, since strictly the Tao is beyond human comprehension. (*Tao Te Ching* 1)

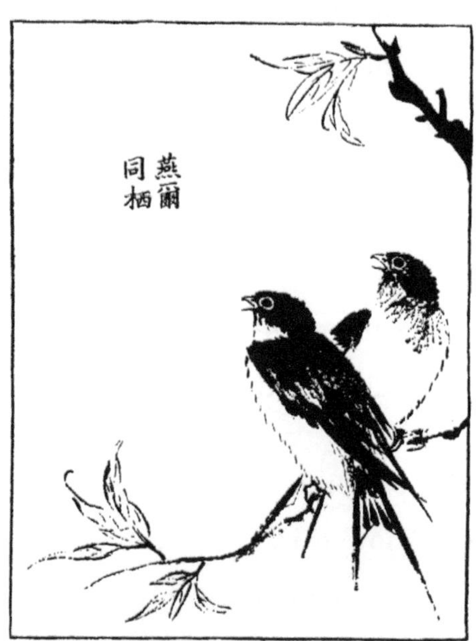

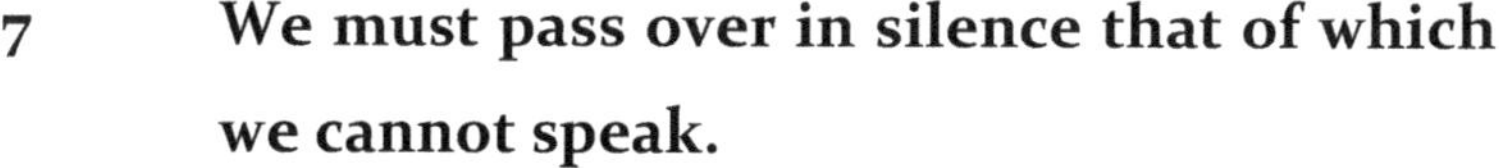

7 We must pass over in silence that of which we cannot speak.

7.1 To speak little is natural. (*Tao Te Ching* 23)

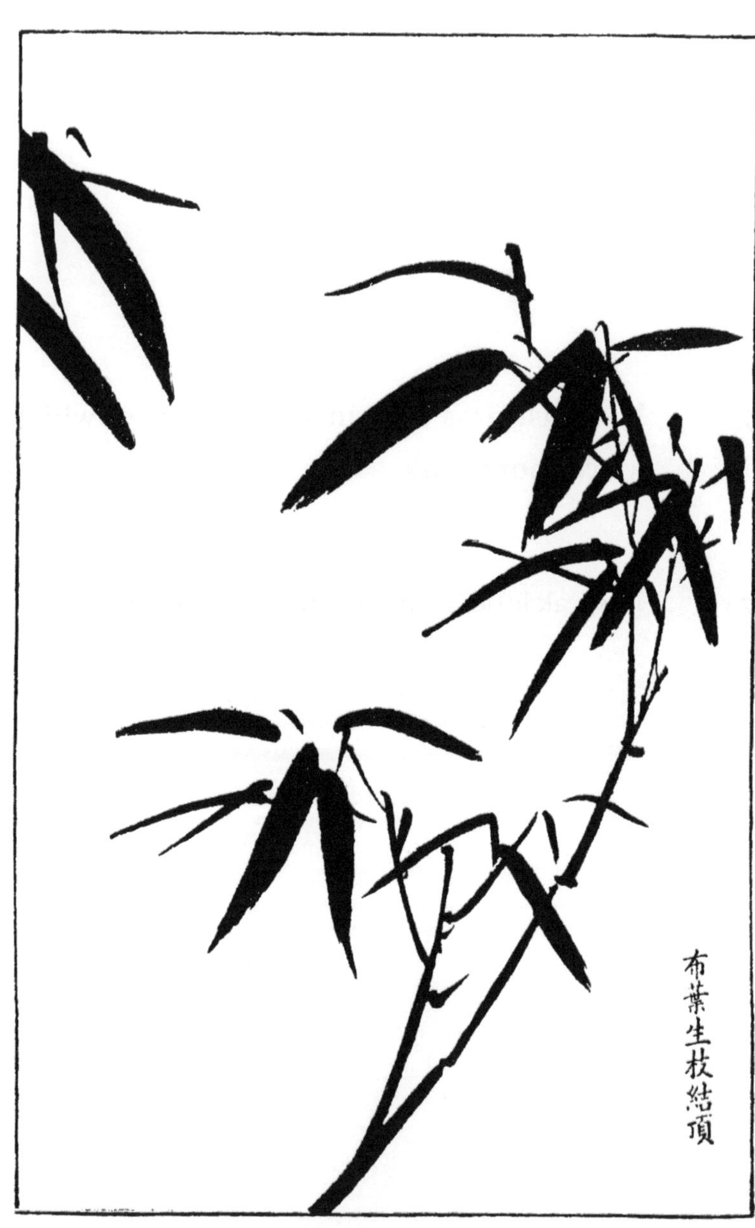
布葉生枝結頂

BIBLIOGRAPHY

Works marked * contain complete translations of the *Tao Te Ching*. Works marked † contain abridged translations, or a selection of chapters from the *Tao Te Ching*.

* Addiss, Stephen and Stanley Lombardo. 1993. *Lao-tzu: Tao Te Ching*. Indianapolis: Hackett.

Allinson, Robert E. 1989. *Chuang-Tzu for Spiritual Transformation: An Analysis of the Inner Chapers*. Albany, NY: State University of New York Press.

* Ames, Roger T. and David L. Hall. 2003. *Daodejing "Making this Life Significant": A Philosophical Translation*. New York: Ballantine Books.

Billington, Ray. 1990. *East of Existentialism: The Tao of the West*. London: Unwin Hyman.

* Carus, Paul. 1898. *Lao-tze's Tao-Teh-King*. Chicago: Open Court.

* ——— and D. T. Suzuki. 1974 [1913]. *The Canon of Reason and Virtue (Lao-Tzu's Tao The King)*. La Salle: Open Court.

Chan, Alan K. L. 1991. *Two Visions of the Way: A Study of the Wang Pi and the Ho-shang Kung Commentaries on the* Lao-Tzu. Albany, NY: State University of New York Press.

Chan, Wing-tsit. 1967a. Chinese philosophy, in Edwards 1967.

———. 1967b. Confucius, in Edwards 1967.

———. 1967c. Chuang Tzu, in Edwards 1967.

———. 1967d. Lao Tzu, in Edwards 1967.

* ———. 1969. *A Source Book in Chinese Philosophy*. Princeton, NJ: Princeton University Press.

Chang Chung-yuan. 1963. *Creativity and Taoism*. New York: Harper & Row.

* Chen, Ellen M. 1989. *The Tao Te Ching: A New Translation with Commentary*. New York: Paragon House.

* Cheng, Man-jan. 1981. *Lao-Tzu: 'My Words Are Very Easy to Understand'*. trans. Tam C. Gibbs. Richmond, CA: North Atlantic Books.

* Ch'en Ku-ying. 1977. *Lao Tzu: Text, Notes, and Commentary*. trans. Rhett Y. W. Young and Roger T. Ames. San Francisco: Chinese Materials Centre.

* Ch'u Ta-Kao. 1985 [1959]. *Tao Tê Ching*. London: Mandala Books.

Cleary, T. 1986. *The Taoist I Ching*. Boston: Shambhala.

———. 1988. *Awakening to the Tao* (Liu I-ming). Boston: Shambhala.

———. 1991. *Wen-tzu: Understanding the Mysteries* (Lao-tzu). Boston: Shambhala.

———. 1992a. *The Essential Confucius*. New York: HarperCollins.

* ———. 1992b. *The Essential Tao*. New York: HarperCollins.

Cooper, J. C. 1981. *Yin & Yang: The Taoist Harmony of Opposites*. Wellingborough: Aquarian Press.

———. 1990. *Taoism: the Way of the Mystic*. Wellingborough: Aquarian Press.

Creel, H. G. 1982. *What is Taoism?* Chicago: University of Chicago Press.

* Dalton, Jerry O. 1994. *Backward Down the Path: A New Approach to the Tao Te Ching*. Atlanta: Humanics New Age.

Daoren, Huanchu. 1990. *Back to Beginnings: Reflections on the Tao*. trans. Thomas Cleary. Boston: Shambhala.

Dawson, R. 1981. *Confucius*. Oxford: Oxford University Press.

———. 1984. *A New Introduction to Classical Chinese*. Oxford: Clardendon Press.

Dreher, Diane. 1990. *The Tao of Peace*. London: Mandala.

* Duyvendak, J. J. L. 1992 [1954]. *Tao Te Ching: The Book of the Way and Its Virtue*. London: John Murray.

Eichhorn, W. 1977. Taoism, in Zaehner 1977.

Edwards, P. ed. 1967. *The Encyclopedia of Philosophy*. New York: Macmillan.

* Feng, Gia-Fu and J. English. 1973. *Lao Tsu: Tao Te Ching*. London: Wildwood House.

———. 1974. *Chuang Tsu: Inner Chapters*. New York: Vintage Books.

* Freke, Timothy. 1995. *Lao Tzu's Tao Te Ching*. London: Piatkus.

† Fung Yu-lan. 1983. *A History of Chinese Philosophy*. Vol. 1. trans. Derk Bodde. Princeton, NJ: Princeton University Press.

Giles, Herbert A. 1926. *Chuang Tzŭ: Taoist Philosopher and Chinese Mystic*. 2nd ed. London: George Allen & Unwin.

Graham, A. C. 1981. *Chuang-Tzŭ: The Inner Chapters*. London: George Allen & Unwin.

———. 1986. *Studies in Chinese Philosophy and Philosophical Literature*. Albany, NY: State University of New York Press.

———. 1989. *Disputers of the Tao*. La Salle: Open Court.

———. 1990. *The Book of Lieh-tzŭ*. New York: Columbia University Press.

———. 1992. *Unreason Within Reason: Essays on the Outskirts of Rationality*. La Salle: Open Court.

* Grigg, Ray. 1995. *The New Lao Tzu: A Comtemporary Tao Te Ching*. Boston, Rutland & Tokyo: Tuttle.

* Henricks, Robert G. 1990. *Lao-Tzu: Te-Tao Ching*. London: Bodley Head.

Herbert, Edward. 1992 [1951]. *A Confucian Notebook*. London: John Murray.

Hinnells, J. R. ed. 1984. *Dictionary of Religions*. Harmondsworth: Penguin.

† Hoff, Benjamin. 1981. *The Way to Life*. New York & Tokyo: John Weatherhill.

———. 1982. *The Tao of Pooh*. London: Methuen.

———. 1992. *The Te of Piglet*. London: Methuen.

† Hughes, E. R. 1942. *Chinese Philosophy in Classical Times*. London: Dent.

Ivanhoe, Philip J. 2000. *Confucian Moral Self Cultivation*. 2nd ed. Indianapolis: Hackett.

* ———. 2002. *The Daodejing of Laozi*. New York: Seven Bridges Press.

* Jiyu, Ren. 1993. *The Book of Lao Zi*. Beijing: Foreign Languages Press.

† Kaltenmark, M. 1969. *Lao Tzu and Taoism*. trans. Roger Greaves. Stanford, CA: Stanford University Press.

* Karlgren, Bernhard. 1975. *Notes on Lao Tse*. reprinted from The Museum of Far Eastern Antiquities: Bulletin No. 47, Stockholm.

Kjellberg, Paul and Philip J. Ivanhoe, eds. 1996. *Essays on Skepticism, Relativism, and Ethics in the Zhuangzi*. Albany, NY: State University Press of New York.

* Kwok, Man-ho, Martin Palmer, Jay Ramsay. 1993. *Tao Te Ching: A New Translation*. Shaftesbury: Element.

* Lao Tzu. 1983. *Tao Te Ching*. trans. anon. Santa Barbara: Concord Grove Press.

* LaFargue, Michael. 1994. *Tao and Method: A Reasoned Approach to the Tao Te Ching*. Albany, NY: State University of New York Press.

Lau, D. C. 1963. *Lao Tzu: Tao Te Ching*. London: Penguin.

———. 1979. *The Analects* (Confucius). Harmondsworth: Penguin.

* ———. 1982. *Tao Te Ching*. Hong Kong: Chinese University Press.

* Legge, J. 1962 [1891]. *The Texts of Taoism*. 2 vols. New York: Dover.

* Lin, P. J. 1977. *A Translation of Lao Tzu's Tao Te Ching and Wang Pi's Commentary*. Ann Arbor: Center for Chinese Studies, University of Michigan.

Lin Yutang. 1938. *The Importance of Living*. London: Heinemann.

* ———. 1958. *The Wisdom of Laotse*. New York: Random House.

Loy Ching-yuen. 1990. *The Book of the Heart: Embracing the Tao*. trans. Trevor Cardan and Bella Chen. Boston & London: Shambhala.

Mair, Victor H. ed. 1983. *Experimental Essays on Chuang-tzu*. Hawaii: Asian Studies at Hawaii, No. 29. University of Hawaii Press.

* ———. 1990. *Tao Te Ching: The Classic Book of Integrity and the Way*. New York: Bantam Books.

* Maurer, H. 1986. *Tao: The Way of the Ways*. Aldershot: Wildwood House.

* Mears, I. 1922. *Tao Teh King by Lao Tzu*. London: Theosophical Publishing House.

Merton, Thomas. 1969. *The Way of Chuang Tzu*. New York: New Directions.

* Metz, Pamela K. 1994. *The Tao of Learning: Lao Tzu's Tao Te Ching Adapted for a New Age*. Atlanta: Humanics New Age.

* Miles, Thomas H. 1992. *Tao Te Ching, Lao Tzu: About the Way of Nature and Its Powers*. New York: Avery Publishing.

* Mitchell, Stephen. 1988. *The Tao Te Ching of Lao Tzu*. London: Macmillan.

Morgan, Evan. 1974. *Tao The Great Luminant: Essays from the Huai Nan Tzu*. Taipei: Ch'eng Wen Publishing Co.

* Ni, Hua-Ching. 1979. *The Complete Works of Lao Tzu*. Malibu, CA: The Shrine of the Eternal Breath of Tao.

Palmer, Martin. 1996. *The Book of Chuang Tzu*. London: Penguin.

* Roberts, Moss. 2001. *Dao De Jing: The Book of the Way*. Berkeley: University of California Press.

Roth, Harold D. 1991. Psychology and self-cultivation in early Taoist thought. *Harvard Journal of Asiatic Studies* 51: 599–650.

* Rump, Ariane and Wing-tsit Chan. 1979. *Commentary on the Lao Tzu by Wang Pi*. Honolulu: University of Hawaii Press.

Schuhmacher, Stephan and Gert Woerner. 1989. *The Rider Encyclopedia of Eastern Philosophy and Religion*. London: Rider.

* Seddon, Keith. 2006. *Lao Tzu: Tao Te Ching*. Morrisville: Lulu.

———. 2006. *Learning the Tao: Chuang Tzu as Teacher*. Morrisville. Lulu.

* Shaman flowing Hands. 1992. *Lao Tzu: Dao Te King*. Penzance: Daoist Foundation.

Siklós, B. 1988. Philosophical and religious Taoism, in Sutherland 1988.

Smart, N. 1971. *The Religious Experience of Mankind*. London: Fontana.

† Smith, D. Howard. 1980. *The Wisdom of the Taoist Masters*. London: Sheldon Press.

Smullyan, Raymond M. 1977. *The Tao is Silent*. New York: Harper & Row.

* Star, Jonathan. 2001. *Tao Te Ching: The Definitive Edition*: New York: Tarcher/Putnam.

Sutherland, S. ed. 1988. *The World's Religions*. London: Routledge.

† Tsai Chih Chung. 1989. *The Sayings of Lao Zi*. trans. Koh Kok Kiang and Wong Lit Khiong. Singapore: Asiapac Books.

† ———. 1992. *The Sayings of Lao Zi: Book 2*. trans. Koh Kok Kiang. Singapore: Asiapac Books.

———. 1992. *Zhuangzi Speaks: The Music of Nature*. trans. Brian Bruya. Princeton, NJ: Princeton University Press.

* Waley, A. 1977 [1934]. *The Way and its Power*. London: Unwin.

———. 1982 [1939]. *Three Ways of Thought in Ancient China*. Stanford, CA: Stanford University Press.

Watson, Burton. 1964. *Chuang Tzu: Basic Writings*. New York: Columbia University Press. [Contains the seven 'Inner Chapters' plus Chapters 17, 18, 19 and 26.]

———. 1968. *The Complete Works of Chuang Tzu*. New York: Columbia University Press.

Watts, Alan. 1992 [1975]. *Tao: The Watercourse Way*. London: Arkana.

Welch, Holmes. 1966. *Taoism: The Parting of the Way*. Boston: Beacon Press.

Wieger, Léon. 1965 [1927]. *Chinese Characters*. New York: Dover.

* ———. 1984. *Wisdom of the Daoist Masters*. trans. Derek Bryce. Lampeter: Llanerch Enterprises.

† ———. 1988. *Philosophy and Religion in China*. trans. Derek Bryce. Lampeter: Llanerch Enterprises.

* ———. 1991. *Lao-Tzu: Tao-Te-Ching*. trans. Derek Bryce. Felinfach: Llanerch Publishers.

———. 1992. *Lieh-tzu*. trans. Derek Bryce. Felinfach: Llanerch Publishers.

* Wilhelm, Richard. 1985. *Tao Te Ching: The Book of Meaning*. trans. H. G. Ostwald. London: Arkana.

* Wing, R. L. 1986. *The Tao of Power*. Wellingborough: Aquarian Press.

* Wu, John C. H. 1989. *Lao Tzu: Tao Teh Ching*. Boston & Shaftesbury: Shambhala.

Wu, Kuang-ming. 1982. *Chuang Tzu: World Philosopher at Play*. New York & Chico: Crossroad and Scholars Press.

———. 1990. *The Butterfly as Companion: Meditations on the first Three Chapters of the Chuang Tzu*. Albany, NY: State University of New York Press.

* Wu, Yi. 1989. *The Book of Lao Tzu (the Tao Te Ching)*. San Francisco: Great Learning Publishing.

Zaehner, R. C. ed. 1977. *The Concise Encyclopedia of Living Faiths*. London: Hutchinson.

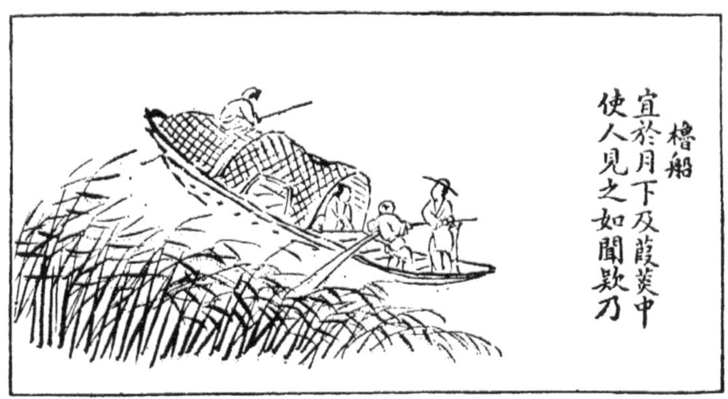

Tractatus Philosophicus Tao

Keith Seddon

first published by Keith Seddon at Lulu 2008

ISBN 978–0–955–68445–6

Typeset in Constantia and Calibri by the author using Microsoft Word 2007. Proofs checked and reviewed in Portable Document Format created using Nitro PDF 4.91.

NOTE ON THE TYPEFACES

Cover text, display text, and running headers are set in Microsoft Calibri, designed by Luc(as) de Groot

Designer's description: 'Calibri is a modern sans serif family with subtle roundings on stems and corners. It features real italics, smallcaps, and multiple numeral sets. Its proportions allow high impact in tightly set lines of big and small text alike. Calibri's many curves and the new rasterizer team up in bigger sizes to reveal a warm and soft character. This font is suitable for documents, email, web design, and magazines.'

(http://www.microsoft.com/typography/ctfonts/CalibriPoster.xps)

Main text is set in Microsoft Constantia, designed by John Hudson

Microsoft informs us: 'Constantia is a modulated wedge-serif typeface designed primarily for continuous text in both electronic and paper publishing. The design responds to the recent narrowing of the gap between screen readability and traditional print media, exploiting specific aspects of the most recent advances in ClearType rendering, such as subpixel positioning. The classic proportions of relatively small x-height and long extenders make Constantia ideal for book and journal publishing, while the slight squareness and open counters ensure that it remains legible even at small sizes. This font is suitable for book typesetting, email, web design, and magazines.'

(http://www.microsoft.com/typography/ctfonts/ConstantiaPoster.xps)

THE ILLUSTRATIONS

The illustrations in this book are taken from *The Mustard Seed Garden Manual of Painting*, Princeton University Press, 1977, certified by the publisher in 1995 as being in the public domain.